T0096818

About the
Urban Land Institute

The mission of the Urban Land Institute is to provide leadership in the responsible use of land and in creating and sustaining thriving communities worldwide. ULI is committed to

- Bringing together leaders from across the fields of real estate and land use policy to exchange best practices and serve community needs;

- Fostering collaboration within and beyond ULI's membership through mentoring, dialogue, and problem solving;

- Exploring issues of urbanization, conservation, regeneration, land use, capital formation, and sustainable development;

- Advancing land use policies and design practices that respect the uniqueness of both the built and natural environments;

- Sharing knowledge through education, applied research, publishing, and electronic media; and

- Sustaining a diverse global network of local practice and advisory efforts that address current and future challenges.

Established in 1936, the Institute today has nearly 30,000 members worldwide, representing the entire spectrum of the land use and development disciplines. ULI relies heavily on the experience of its members. It is through member involvement and information resources that ULI has been able to set standards of excellence in development practice. The Institute has long been recognized as one of the world's most respected and widely quoted sources of objective information on urban planning, growth, and development.

Recommended bibliographic listing:
Lachman, M. Leanne, and Deborah L. Brett. *Generation Y: Shopping and Entertainment in the Digital Age.* Washington, D.C.: Urban Land Institute, 2013.

ISBN: 978-0-87420-279-3

Copyright 2013 by the Urban Land Institute
1025 Thomas Jefferson Street, NW
Suite 500 West
Washington, DC 20007-5201

About the Authors

M. Leanne Lachman is president of Lachman Associates, a real estate consulting firm serving private and institutional investors. She is also an executive-in-residence at Columbia University's Graduate Business School and serves on the boards of Liberty Property Trust and Lincoln National Corporation.

After an early career in market analysis with Real Estate Research Corporation, where she was president and chief executive officer for eight years and initiated the *Emerging Trends in Real Estate* publication, Lachman moved into portfolio management for pension funds. She spent 13 years as a partner with Schroder Real Estate Associates, which was sold to Lend Lease Real Estate Investments, where she was head of real estate strategies.

Lachman is widely published and is a frequent speaker. She is a ULI trustee and governor; is listed in *Who's Who in America*, *Who's Who in Finance and Industry*, and *The World Who's Who of Women*; and received the James Graaskamp Award for pragmatic real estate research in 1997 from the Pension Real Estate Association. She was awarded a BA from the University of Southern California and an MA from Claremont Graduate University.

Deborah L. Brett is a real estate and planning consultant for a wide range of public and private organizations, providing project-related market analyses. Areas of specialization include development planning, commercial revitalization, market-rate and affordable housing, mixed-use projects, and transit-oriented development.

Brett formed Deborah L. Brett & Associates, based in Plainsboro, New Jersey, in 1993. She previously served as senior vice president and director of consulting services at Real Estate Research Corporation in Chicago. In her 18-year career there, she directed land use policy studies for many government agencies and prepared development strategies and analyses for private clients.

Brett holds a master's degree in urban and regional planning from the University of Illinois at Urbana-Champaign. She is a longtime member of ULI and a frequent contributor to its publications, including *Real Estate Market Analysis: Methods and Case Studies*, used by real estate and planning programs at many universities. Brett is also a member of the American Institute of Certified Planners and Lambda Alpha, the real estate and land economics honorary society.

Dr. Lawrence Becker provided assistance in survey design, sampling, and statistical analysis. He holds a PhD in social psychology from the University of California at Davis and has extensive experience in market and advertising research.

Letter

Dear Reader:

Demographics continue to fascinate. As the U.S. economic recovery settles in and struggles for firm footing, market participants reflect on what various age cohorts will need and want. Of particular interest is the Generation Y/Millennial population, now 18 to 35 years of age and the largest age cohort in American history. This group has been slow to marry and slow to become financially independent and espouses less interest in "worldly" goods. Is this a function of the aftermath of the Great Recession, a fundamental change in values, or their difficulties in finding well-paying jobs? About 80 million in size, this group constitutes more than 25 percent of the U.S. population. What the Millennials do and how they consume will affect the economy—and real estate—in material ways.

The Urban Land Institute has taken a special interest in Gen Y, given its size and the market uncertainty about how members of this age cohort will move into the full economy. In 2010, the Institute commissioned a study led by M. Leanne Lachman and Deborah L. Brett, *Generation Y: America's New Housing Wave*. A statistically accurate survey aligned to the 2010 census, the study produced results indicating that while Gen Y may be slow to jump into homeownership en masse, a full 35 percent of the members of this generation already own homes and a robust 82 percent expect to own homes by 2015. While this may prove optimistic in light of today's tight lending requirements and hefty downpayment needs, Gen Y looks to both follow and change some housing assumptions relative to urban and suburban residential patterns.

The success of the Gen Y housing study suggested that ULI explore Gen Y and retail patterns. Retail is undergoing both good times and bad. While "creative destruction" is shaking up the industry and causing closures and repositioning, retail has remained surprisingly strong over the past five years. The retail real estate mix continues to evolve as seen in power centers, traditional malls, and lifestyle centers. Internet sales, instant access to product reviews, fashion blogs, and continuous sales information are challenging all retailers and offering shoppers more information than ever before. What to make of it all?

This study, *Generation Y: Shopping and Entertainment in the Digital Age*, is based on a representative sample of American Gen Y consumers. Of greatest interest to the real estate community is Millennials' enthusiasm for shopping in all its forms. Shopping is seen as entertainment and is done alone as well as with family and friends. It is clearly an extension of the social network. Gen Y seeks out high stimulation, requiring retail venues to stay on top of changing trends and regularly upgrade their facilities and offerings. The competition is fierce and the best are getting better. A dizzying array of tools now allows retailers to stay in touch with consumers and track preferences.

We hope this publication will again spur lively dialogue and interest across all ULI platforms and networks. Retail affects the liveliness of place, and contributes to the urbanization of suburban town centers as well as to the revitalization of downtown cores. Often critical to the success of mixed-use developments, retail is the front face of many of our projects and core to community building.

I would like to particularly thank John Bucksbaum and the Bucksbaum family for their generous support of this study.

Patrick L. Phillips
Chief Executive Officer
Urban Land Institute

Contents

Generation Y:
Shopping and Entertainment in the Digital Age

Great news for retail real estate owners: Generation Y thoroughly enjoys shopping and frequently visits most types of centers. However, the challenging corollary is that 18- to 35-year-olds are bored easily, so they're on the lookout for new excitement—online, in brick-and-mortar settings, and in restaurants. Sensory aspects of retail facilities need to evolve constantly in order to retain young shoppers' patronage.

In January 2013, ULI and Lachman Associates conducted a nationally representative online survey of 1,251 Gen-Yers to gauge their retail, dining, and entertainment preferences.[1] The survey design reflects the results of a focus group conducted at Columbia University's Graduate School of Business in Manhattan, as well as a search of the literature on Gen Y's shopping habits and free-time activities. The two-page spread (figure 2) that begins on page 2 illustrates the survey respondents' demographics, and detailed findings are presented in the body of this monograph. This section addresses real estate implications of the survey results.

Key Findings

Figure 1 breaks down Gen Y's viewpoint: 37 percent love shopping, another 48 percent enjoy it, and 12 percent view it as a chore but can cope with it; only 4 percent hate to shop. Half the men and 70 percent of the women consider shopping a form of entertainment and something to share with friends and family. Importantly, that is an aspect of shopping that

FIGURE 1: Attitudes about Shopping

	Love to shop	Shop when necessary, and I enjoy it	Shopping is a necessary chore; I can deal with it	Hate shopping
Total sample	**37%**	**48%**	**12%**	**4%**
Men	29%	51%	15%	5%
Women	44%	45%	9%	3%
Hispanic	44%	45%	8%	3%
Non-Hispanic	35%	48%	12%	4%
White	33%	50%	12%	5%
Black	55%	34%	8%	3%
Other[1]	32%	50%	17%	1%

Sample size: 1,251.

Source: ULI/Lachman Associates Survey, January 2013.

Note: Totals may not add up to 100 percent because of rounding.

1. Other includes Asians, Native Americans, Pacific Islanders, and people who identify themselves as biracial or multiracial.

FIGURE 2: Profile of Surveyed Gen-Yers

	Percentage of total sample			Percentage of total sample
Gender			**Marital status**	
Male	49%		Single	64%
Female	51%		Divorced or widowed	2%
Age			Married	34%
18–25	45%		**Living with children under age 18**	
26–30	27%		Yes	37%
31–35	28%		No	63%
Race			**Have a car**	
White	74%		Yes	76%
Black	16%		No	24%
Other[1]	10%		**Pet owner**	
Hispanic origin			Yes	71%
Yes	20%		No	29%
No	80%			

	Percentage of total sample
Educational attainment	
No high school diploma	9%
High school graduate	19%
Some college, trade school, apprenticeship	37%
Bachelor's degree	22%
Postgraduate study/advanced degree	13%
Parental contribution to living expenses	
None	65%
Under 25%	9%
25%–49%	10%
50%–100%	16%

Sample size: 1,251, except Gen-Yers' Household Income—sample size: 1,166.

Source: ULI/Lachman Associates Survey, January 2013.
Note: Totals may not add up to 100 percent because of rounding.
1. Other includes Asians, Native Americans, Pacific Islanders, and people who identify themselves as biracial or multiracial.

Current Housing

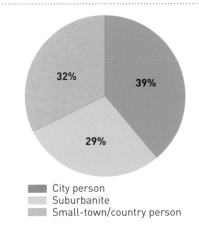

- 32% Own
- 37% Rent
- 24% Live with family
- 2% Student housing
- 5% Other

Gen-Yers' Household Income

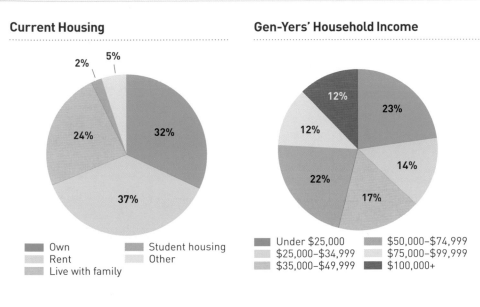

- 23% Under $25,000
- 14% $25,000–$34,999
- 17% $35,000–$49,999
- 22% $50,000–$74,999
- 12% $75,000–$99,999
- 12% $100,000+

Gen Y's Self-Image

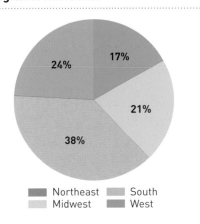

- 39% City person
- 29% Suburbanite
- 32% Small-town/country person

Region of Residence

- 17% Northeast
- 21% Midwest
- 38% South
- 24% West

Employment Status

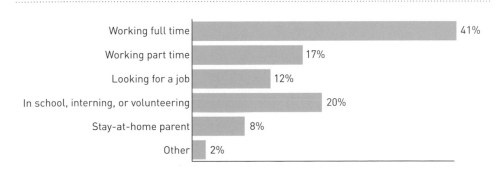

- Working full time — 41%
- Working part time — 17%
- Looking for a job — 12%
- In school, interning, or volunteering — 20%
- Stay-at-home parent — 8%
- Other — 2%

cannot be replicated easily online—though pinterest.com, Skype, and social media are encroaching on face-to-face interactions. More women than men love to shop, but most young men find it enjoyable and are engaged. More Hispanics than non-Hispanics love shopping, as do more blacks than whites.

Over half of all Gen-Yers go at least once a month to the following retail formats:

- discount department stores (91 percent);
- neighborhood and community shopping centers (74 percent);
- enclosed malls (64 percent);
- full-line department stores (64 percent);
- big-box power centers (63 percent);
- chain apparel stores (58 percent); and
- neighborhood business districts (54 percent).

At the same time, though, 91 percent of Gen Y made online purchases over the previous six months, and 45 percent spend more than an hour per day looking at retail-oriented websites. They are researching products, comparing prices, envisioning how clothing or accessories would look on them, or responding to flash sales or coupon offers. In terms of actual purchasing, stores still dominate; but Gen-Yers are multichannel shoppers.

Gen-Yers are big fans of eating out: 46 percent dine at least weekly with friends or family outside their homes; one-quarter do so several times each week, with dinner being slightly more popular than lunch. Many are serious foodies, and 25 percent say they grocery shop more than once a week; another 40 percent shop weekly for groceries.

Survey details will be of interest to many real estate owners, operators, and developers, who will see implications for their properties. A few key conclusions follow.

1. Warehousing and logistics are the big winners in omni-channel retailing. E-commerce requires pick-and-pack operations, which are structured differently than distribution warehouses, but both are in demand. Tenants will come and go as various retailers experiment with different methods of online and in-store fulfillment in search of cost efficiencies and ever-faster deliveries.

2. Gen Y strongly supports discount department stores and warehouse clubs, which could expand in all geographies. Smaller formats may suit infill sites, and municipal governments should be encouraging this type of development. Mall owners with vacant space might consider these stores as well.

3. Enclosed malls remain popular, but it will take work to retain their appeal among fickle Gen Y. Suggestions include the following:

   - Refresh interiors frequently with paint, lighting, new carts, etc.
   - Encourage social gathering—in food courts, center courts, restaurants, and temporary or permanent event venues.
   - Keep those pop-up stores popping up. They're great for testing new formats, some of which will become permanent.
   - Add specialty food purveyors and grocery stores.

- Incorporate movie theaters—and renovate obsolete ones.

- Become pickup/drop-off points for merchandise ordered online. As retailers move to multichannel selling, with tight integration among in-store, online, and social networking experiences, shopping centers can do the same.

4. Restaurants at all price points are popular, but beware of paying high tenant improvement allowances to attract them. Young consumers want to move from one hot spot to another, and only very deep markets can sustain that kind of transience; in most places, "hot" turns cold and then becomes vacant.

5. America's chronically excessive inventory of retail space is worsening. Smaller formats are more suitable for time-conscious shoppers, many of whom may just be "showrooming"—looking at goods they will ultimately buy online. Also, the third and fourth regional malls in a market are unlikely to be able to offer the "excitement factor" that Gen Y demands. It is time for redevelopment, possibly with multiple, denser uses.

6. For both urban and suburban Gen-Yers, the ideal is to walk or bike to the market, drugstores, the gym, the ATM, coffeehouses, and restaurants. Denser, pedestrian-friendly development will appeal to Gen Y.

7. Most of today's lifestyle centers target older, more affluent shoppers. Yet the format also suits Gen Y. Owners and developers might consider the following:

   - a broader choice of eateries;

   - apparel brands favored by Gen Y (such as J. Crew, Old Navy, Forever 21, H&M, Zara);

   - a gym;

   - hair/blow-dry salons;

   - Trader Joe's and green grocers;

   - a bike shop;

   - a pet store and/or a dog run; or

   - uniquely local offerings.

8. Power centers are problematic because one big-box category after another is being put out of business by the internet. Aggregators like Amazon.com and Soap.com are what big boxes were in the 1980s. Discount department stores and warehouse clubs are Gen-Y favorites, but many power centers will lose some of their other tenants and be forced to downsize or substitute nonretail uses.

9. Increased retail focus will be on underserved communities, whether in central cities or in smaller towns and rural areas. Target, Walmart Express, and Aldi recognize this opportunity and are introducing ruthlessly productive formats that will do well. Again, both developers and municipal planning departments should capitalize on these opportunities.

10. More "third places" are needed—indoor and outdoor venues where folks can safely linger for a while, meet others, go online, and network. Starbucks and wi-fi parks are models, but more are needed—public libraries, juice bars at gyms, food courts, office building ground floors, plazas and gardens with seating, and, certainly, enclosed malls.

Where Gen Y Lives

When asked how they describe their residential orientation, 39 percent of Gen-Yers said they are "city" people, as shown in figure 2. This is higher than the 33 percent found in the summer 2010 Gen-Y survey.[2] Among current respondents in their 30s, only 34 percent say they are city people versus 41 percent of those 18 to 30. It's cool to live in the heart of the city, even if you are not going to stay forever. Significantly, 54 percent of Hispanics and 63 percent of blacks describe themselves as city folks; we assume most of them grew up in cities In other words, one should not conclude that all the "city" types migrate there: many simply stay where they were raised.

Whereas 29 percent of all respondents claim to be "suburbanites," only 22 percent of Hispanics and blacks use that descriptor. Among Gen-Yers in their 30s, 36 percent identify with the suburbs, and those folks have the highest homeownership rate in the sample. One-third of Gen Y says they are "small-town/country people." Among whites, the proportion is 37 percent; but it is a much lower 25 percent for Hispanics and just 17 percent for blacks.

FIGURE 3: Where Gen Y Lives

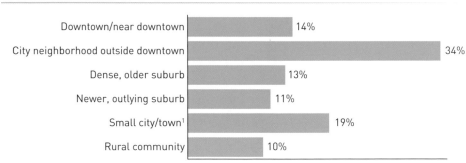

Downtown/near downtown — 14%
City neighborhood outside downtown — 34%
Dense, older suburb — 13%
Newer, outlying suburb — 11%
Small city/town[1] — 19%
Rural community — 10%

Sample size: 1,251.

Source: ULI/Lachman Associates Survey, January 2013.
Note: Totals may not add up to 100 percent because of rounding.
1. Population under 50,000.

Locational self-images do not necessarily match respondents' current places of residence, which are graphed in figure 3. In contrast to the 39 percent who define themselves as city people, nearly 48 percent actually live in cities: 14 percent in or near downtowns, but a much larger 34 percent in other urban neighborhoods. Although a relatively small share of the total sample, "downtowners" are a unique lot, varying from their Gen-Y peers in numerous statistically significant ways:

- 62 percent are male, compared with 47 percent of all other respondents.
- 51 percent are age 18 to 25 versus 44 percent for the rest of the sample.
- 34 percent are Hispanic, compared with 18 percent of others.
- 23 percent are black versus 15 percent of those not living downtown.

- "Downtowners" comprise 20 percent of Gen Yers residing in the Northeast, compared with only 10 percent of those living in the South.

- As Gen Y's fashionistas, downtowners shop far more frequently—in all types of centers and stores. They are inveterate patrons of department stores, chain apparel retailers, and upscale boutiques.

- 14 percent buy groceries daily versus 6 percent of all respondents.

- 21 percent frequent green grocers/farmers markets for fresh foods, as compared with 16 percent of the total sample.

Demographically, nondowntown city residents are similar to those in dense, older suburbs.

Among Hispanics, 56 percent live in cities, as do 59 percent of blacks.

In total, 23 percent of survey respondents live in suburbs, 19 percent are in small cities and towns with fewer than 50,000 residents, and 10 percent reside in rural areas. This profile is important in understanding Gen Y's shopping habits and their stated preferences among types of malls and stores: retail choices are often limited outside of major markets, as well as in lower-income urban and older suburban neighborhoods.

Gen Y's Finances

According to a recent essay published in the *New York Times Magazine*, Gen Y's "relationship with money seems quite simple. They do not have a lot of it, and what they do have, they seem reluctant to spend."[3] That assertion, however, is not borne out by our survey. As portrayed in the summary, more than 45 percent of our respondents have annual household incomes exceeding $50,000, and the median is $45,979. For 18- to 35-year-olds, this is not bad, especially given that one-quarter of them still live with parents and/or other older relatives and many are in school and not working full time. In addition, some of those who live independently receive financial assistance from parents, as discussed later.

American Express and the Harrison Group, a Connecticut-based marketing consulting firm, observe that one-third of Gen Y grew up relatively wealthy. The Ipsos Mendelsohn Affluent Survey found that 11.8 million Millennials age 18 to 30 live in households with incomes exceeding $100,000 per year.[4] (Many of these young people are still at home with their families.) People who grow up in financial comfort typically are not driven by money or traditional status symbols. At the same time, Gen Y respects quality of materials and manufacture: casual is fine, but so is a designer hoodie! Similarly, Gen-Yers might patronize Walmart but wear a Zegna tie or Manolo Blahnik shoes. They will travel to the World Cup in South Africa or Brazil but shop at Sam's Club.

Only two out of five survey respondents have full-time jobs; but among those who do, the median reported income is $49,612. One-quarter earn less than $35,000, while 22 percent make in excess of $75,000. Of the total sample, 17 percent work part time, and 12 percent are looking for jobs. One-third of the sample are in school, interning, or volunteering.

Forty percent of survey respondents never had any student debt, and another 11 percent repaid everything they had borrowed. Of the 49 percent with outstanding student loans, about one-third owe less than $15,000. The median unpaid loan balance is $23,370.[5] That said, almost one-quarter of those carrying student debt have outstanding balances exceeding $50,000. This limits borrowers' ability to spend freely on retail purchases and entertainment.

Gen Y's credit card debt is modest. Among survey respondents, 38 percent do not use credit cards at all, and an additional 27 percent pay their balance in full each month. Half of those who do have credit card debt carry a balance under $3,000; one-quarter have $3,000 to $6,000 in total credit card obligations; and one-quarter are more than $6,000 in debt. Phrased differently, less than 9 percent of Gen-Yers have ongoing credit card debt exceeding $6,000. The Pew Research Center monitors student loan obligations and other debt among U.S. households led by someone under 35 and its findings[6] corroborate ours:

■ Few maintain credit card balances.

■ Median household debt dropped 29 percent—from $22,000 in 2007 to $15,500 in 2010. (The drop among older households was 8 percent.)

■ Debt declined or stabilized for 56 percent of young families.

■ Bankruptcies and foreclosures contributed to debt reduction.

■ In 2010, 40 percent of households headed by someone under 35 had student debt, with $13,410 being the median amount owed.

According to Moody's Analytics, savings rates have risen among young adults—much more than within other age groups.[7]

Our respondents who do *not* use credit cards can be characterized as follows:

■ 58 percent of those under 26 years of age;

■ 25 percent of 26- to 30-year-olds;

■ 18 percent of Gen-Yers in their 30s;

■ 28 percent of Hispanics overall;

■ 48 percent of blacks;

■ 48 percent of small-town residents; and

■ 52 percent of those living in rural areas.

Presumably, these people use debit cards. They buy online, so they clearly have a means of paying for their purchases.

Like other surveys, ours shows 24 percent of respondents living with their parents or other older relatives. Among the youngest age group (18–25), 38 percent live with relatives; for 26- to 30-year-olds, the proportion drops to 15 percent; and just 10 percent of those in their early 30s are living with parents and/or related adults. As highlighted in

the summary, over one-third of Gen-Yers receive contributions from their parents to help with living expenses. After eliminating respondents living at home or in college housing, only 22 percent of independently living Gen-Yers rely on parents for financial help. Of those, however, many get quite a lot of help:

■ Half have their cellphone costs covered (presumably as members of family plans).

■ 36 percent receive contributions toward clothing expenses.

■ 34 percent for car insurance.

■ 33 percent for rent payments and cable bills.

■ 28 percent for gasoline.

■ 28 percent for other durable goods.

■ 23 percent for school tuition/fees.

■ 22 percent for health insurance.

■ 20 percent for out-of-pocket medical costs.

■ 20 percent for car payments.

■ 16 percent for student loan payments.

■ 16 percent for travel/vacations.

These contributions again reflect parents' tight bonds with young adult children. However, it is also true that many Gen-Yers who have completed their educations simply do not earn enough to pay for all the "necessities" they take for granted.

Despite the typical Gen-Yer's thriftiness, 1,165 of our 1,251 survey respondents say they occasionally splurge on retail goods. Their indulgences are not expensive, however. Two-fifths spend less than $50, and another one-fifth say their splurges cost $50 to $75. Only one-fifth blow more than $100. Half say their extravagances are clothes or shoes, and almost 40 percent cite electronics; gifts and personal accessories are each mentioned by one-fourth of Gen-Yers.

Shopping Center Patronage

Shopping center owners can rest easy: Gen-Yers enjoy visiting retail centers and doing so frequently. Neighborhood and community centers receive the most visits because they offer convenience goods in supermarkets, discount department stores, and home improvement centers. Almost two-thirds of survey respondents go to enclosed malls at least once a month, as reflected in figure 4. This applies no matter where they live, with two exceptions: three-fourths of downtowners go at least monthly (28 percent say they are weekly patrons), whereas only 42 percent of rural residents get to enclosed malls once a month—presumably because they must travel farther.

FIGURE 4: Frequency of Shopping Center Visits

	Total	Downtown or near downtown	Other city neighborhood	Dense older suburb	Newer suburb	Small town	Rural
PLACE OF RESIDENCE							
Neighborhood or community shopping center[1]							
At least weekly	21%	25%	23%	18%	18%	18%	23%
A couple of times a month	30%	38%	28%	27%	31%	29%	33%
Once a month	23%	18%	22%	29%	27%	24%	20%
Rarely	21%	15%	23%	21%	19%	23%	17%
Never	5%	4%	5%	6%	5%	6%	7%
Enclosed mall[2]							
At least weekly	14%	28%	13%	9%	14%	10%	11%
A couple of times a month	24%	26%	25%	27%	25%	20%	20%
Once a month	26%	21%	26%	27%	28%	29%	21%
Rarely	33%	21%	33%	35%	32%	37%	42%
Never	3%	3%	3%	3%	1%	5%	6%
Open-air shopping center with big-box stores[3]							
At least weekly	12%	19%	13%	9%	14%	8%	8%
A couple of times a month	26%	31%	26%	26%	25%	22%	27%
Once a month	25%	17%	25%	28%	34%	27%	15%
Rarely	29%	25%	29%	31%	22%	29%	36%
Never	9%	8%	7%	7%	5%	13%	14%
Neighborhood business district							
At least weekly	13%	24%	14%	7%	9%	10%	13%
A couple of times a month	20%	24%	21%	24%	19%	16%	19%
Once a month	21%	19%	22%	18%	29%	20%	17%
Rarely	33%	21%	32%	37%	31%	40%	31%
Never	13%	12%	11%	14%	12%	15%	19%
Downtown business district							
At least weekly	12%	27%	11%	4%	10%	9%	8%
A couple of times a month	18%	27%	18%	16%	16%	13%	21%
Once a month	18%	18%	19%	16%	15%	19%	12%
Rarely	39%	22%	39%	48%	46%	41%	36%
Never	14%	6%	12%	16%	13%	19%	23%
Sample size	*1,251*	*173*	*423*	*160*	*134*	*237*	*134*

Source: ULI/Lachman Associates Survey, January 2013.

Note: Totals may not add up to 100 percent because of rounding.

Definitions:

1. Typically anchored by a supermarket and/or a discount department store or home improvement center.

2. Typically have at least three large anchor stores (generally department stores).

3. Clusters of larger stores, usually open air.

When asked which three aspects of their most visited enclosed malls they like best, Gen Y mentions:

There are lots of options for finding things I want/need	53%
Going to the mall provides a chance to get out	42%
Stores offer styles I like	37%
Stores have items I can afford	33%
Stores sell brands I trust	31%
I like shopping in a climate-controlled environment	29%
There are good places to eat	28%
It is a good place to meet people/hang out	22%

Women tend to emphasize the first four characteristics, whereas men put greater weight on the bottom four, particularly valuing the presence of stores selling brands they trust. Also, 27 percent of men say enclosed malls are good places to meet and hang out versus just 16 percent of women. Younger Gen-Yers enjoy social gatherings at malls twice as much as those over 25. On the other hand, older respondents express greater appreciation for climate-controlled environments.

Gen Y's emphasis on "lots of options" and "styles I like" ties into their continuous search for the latest trend, new sensory experiences, vibes, and fun. Mall owners should take this to heart: it's their competitive advantage over often drab discount department stores. But change must be constant. If a mall—or the stores in it—becomes stale, Gen Y will move on. Novel experiences need not be expensive; for example, mood lighting can come and go, paint is cheap, amateur performers welcome the chance to be seen, and charity activities appeal to Gen Y. Pop-up stores, event venues, and restaurants add novelty and, instead of simply filling temporary spaces, pop-ups can occupy permanent "transit" slots that change periodically so shoppers encounter surprises. If one grew up with video games, movies on demand, YouTube, and Facebook, one is accustomed to being entertained and visually stimulated continuously. Noise and motion are positive, but, if they become too intense, Gen-Yers just insert their ear buds and listen to their own choices. Mall marketing directors need to be forever imaginative—and tweet patrons about what's going on at their centers.

We gave survey respondents an opportunity to identify potential improvements to the enclosed mall they visit most frequently, with each person able to select three items from a list. The most common suggestions are:

Add new clothing or shoe stores	54%
Change store mix in another way	45%
Add more restaurants	43%
Freshen/change decor/atmosphere	42%
Add special events/concerts/exhibits	40%
Bring in grocery or specialty food stores	31%
Redo the food court	27%

Gen Y's notoriety for becoming bored quickly and constantly seeking new experiences is reflected in some of these mall suggestions. However, young patrons are also capable of moving on to the next new thing if their favorite malls and stores become stale. We repeat: retailers and mall owners should take this to heart. Frequent renovations and refreshes are in order to continue to attract Generation Y.

Almost two-thirds of Gen Y—or nearly 50 million shoppers between 18 and 35 years old—visit big-box centers at least once each month. The proportion is closer to three-fourths among residents of newer suburbs, where power centers are prevalent. In contrast, visitation drops for small-town Gen-Yers and is just 50 percent in rural America. Even there, however, only 14 percent say they never shop at big-box centers. Nonetheless, industry observers fear that power centers are most vulnerable to online shopping because they tend to sell commodity items and are susceptible to undercutting of prices. Think Circuit City, Linens 'n Things, Hollywood Video, Comp-USA, Tower Records, Borders, and Kids "R" Us.

Although we asked about lifestyle centers and outlet malls, Gen-Y patronage was infrequent. Lifestyle centers tend to locate in upper-middle-income suburbs, and their store mix skews toward middle-aged and older women with stores like Chico's, Coldwater Creek, Talbots, Easy Spirit, and Clarks. Although their restaurants and casual eateries may appeal to Gen-Yers, these malls did not resonate with survey respondents. Outlet malls are typically found along interstate highways (either between two urban areas or at the suburban fringe) or in tourist destinations, but not in highly developed residential areas. They are infrequent day trip destinations for locals living within 25 to 50 miles. Again, Gen-Yers visit occasionally, but outlets are not prime shopping targets for them.

Nearly 55 percent of Gen-Yers visit neighborhood business districts at least monthly. There is little differentiation across residential locations, except for downtowners, two-thirds of whom go monthly. In fact, one-quarter of downtown residents say they visit a neighborhood business district at least weekly, and another quarter go a couple of times a month. With all the talk about Gen Y favoring walkable communities and nearby conveniences, we expected higher overall patronage of these business districts, which offer coffee shops, pizzerias, locally owned restaurants, banks, and drugstores. However, they include little in the way of comparison shopping.

Not surprisingly, 72 percent of downtown residents go to central business district (CBD) retailers at least monthly—and generally more often. For people living in "other city neighborhoods," almost half visit a downtown business district at least once monthly. Among Gen-Yers in other locales, the proportion is four out of ten; and many say they never visit CBD retail stores. In fact, overall patronage of downtowns is pretty evenly split between those who visit at least monthly and those who rarely or never shop in CBDs.

Store Patronage

In addition to asking about shopping center visits, we queried Gen-Yers about their patronage of specific types of stores. The results are in figure 5.

FIGURE 5: **Frequency of Visits to Various Store Types**

		Total	Downtown or near downtown	Other city neighborhood	Dense older suburb	Newer suburb	Small town	Rural
PLACE OF RESIDENCE								
Discount department store or warehouse club[1]								
At least weekly		31%	24%	33%	29%	36%	29%	36%
A couple of times a month		38%	45%	36%	31%	43%	41%	34%
Once a month		22%	18%	20%	31%	16%	23%	23%
Rarely		9%	10%	11%	9%	5%	7%	6%
Never		1%	2%	1%	1%	0%	0%	1%
Full-line department store[2]								
At least weekly		12%	27%	10%	8%	14%	8%	10%
A couple of times a month		21%	23%	23%	23%	22%	17%	17%
Once a month		31%	24%	32%	26%	35%	34%	31%
Rarely		32%	25%	32%	39%	25%	35%	37%
Never		3%	2%	2%	4%	4%	6%	6%
Apparel-oriented department store[3]								
At least weekly		5%	14%	5%	2%	6%	3%	4%
A couple of times a month		13%	23%	13%	13%	16%	8%	10%
Once a month		19%	24%	16%	23%	22%	19%	15%
Rarely		41%	28%	48%	41%	34%	43%	41%
Never		21%	12%	18%	23%	22%	27%	31%
Chain apparel store[4]								
At least weekly		9%	20%	8%	4%	12%	5%	7%
A couple of times a month		20%	27%	22%	23%	20%	13%	14%
Once a month		29%	27%	27%	31%	28%	33%	27%
Rarely		33%	23%	33%	30%	31%	40%	40%
Never		10%	3%	10%	13%	10%	8%	13%
Upscale or designer apparel store or boutique[5]								
At least weekly		8%	19%	8%	3%	7%	4%	7%
A couple of times a month		11%	16%	11%	11%	13%	9%	5%
Once a month		15%	20%	15%	16%	14%	11%	18%
Rarely		36%	27%	38%	35%	35%	41%	35%
Never		29%	18%	27%	34%	30%	35%	35%
Sample size		*1,251*	*173*	*423*	*160*	*134*	*237*	*134*

Source: ULI/Lachman Associates Survey, January 2013.
Note: Totals may not add up to 100 percent because of rounding.
Definitions:
1. Such as Target, Walmart, Kmart, Costco, Sam's Club, BJ's.
2. Such as Macy's, Sears, JCPenney, Kohl's, Dillard's, Bloomingdale's.
3. Such as Lord & Taylor, Nordstrom, Neiman-Marcus.
4. Such as Gap, Old Navy, H&M, Ann Taylor, Zara, Forever 21, the Limited, Express, Banana Republic, J.Crew, Lane Bryant, etc.
5. Local or chain.

Most popular—and visited at least weekly by 31 percent of Gen-Yers—are discount department stores and warehouse clubs. More than 90 percent go to them once a month or more, and patronage is consistent across all geographies. Discount department stores and warehouse clubs have successfully penetrated urban America, increasingly with smaller infill formats. Nearly nine of ten city residents visit such stores regularly, as do their suburban and rural peers.

"Next time we're shopping at Wal-Mart."

We asked an open-ended question about where respondents go for "trendy" or "chic" clothing items without spending too much. Each person could cite up to three stores or web locations. With 1,251 respondents, the answers were all over the map; however, the most frequent mentions were JCPenney (172), followed closely by Target (166), Walmart (164), and Kohl's (161). Though separate stores, Marshalls (66) and T.J. Maxx (95) are under the same ownership. Macy's gets 139 votes. Old Navy is mentioned by 125 and Forever 21 by 103. Amazon.com garnered 99 votes and Gap got 78.

Nearly two-thirds of Gen-Yers go to a full-line department store at least monthly and one-third visit two or more times. Among small-town and rural residents, almost 60 percent get to a Macy's, Sears, JCPenney, Kohl's, Dillard's, or the like each month. Department stores are far from dead! However, apparel-oriented upscale department stores like Lord & Taylor, Nordstrom, and Neiman-Marcus are less appealing, with 62 percent of respondents saying they rarely or never visit. For most Gen-Y consumers, these stores either do not exist nearby or are considered too pricey. The exception is downtowners; 61 percent of them go to this type of store at least once a month. Again, these folks have unique shopping habits; too bad there aren't more of them.

Moderate- to mid-priced chain apparel stores, on the other hand, are broadly popular—but not as much as full-line department stores. Only 9 percent of Gen Y shops weekly at places like Old Navy, H&M, or Ann Taylor Loft, but 58 percent go once or twice a month. (In contrast, one-third of respondents rarely go to these stores, and another 10 percent say they never do.) The shopping pattern is consistent across residential locations, with the exception of downtowners again: 20 percent of them go to a chain apparel store at least weekly and another 54 percent go once or twice a month. Unlike most Gen-Yers, downtowners are also frequent visitors to designer stores and independent boutiques.

With respect to shopping, good customer service is very important to 48 percent of Gen Y and somewhat important to an additional 48 percent—and this is a pretty universal expectation in all their commercial interactions.

This generation shops with friends and family, as noted in figure 6. When buying clothes, a very high 37 percent typically go with family members and 28 percent shop with friends. Only 35 percent go alone. There are marked differences in these shopping patterns by age. The youngest Gen-Yers, who are most likely to be single, tend to go with friends. The oldest cohort often shops with spouses or partners and may have children tagging along. More of their shopping trips are family centered.

FIGURE 6: When shopping for clothes, do you typically . . . ?

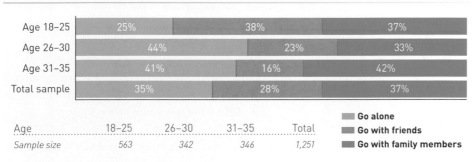

Age	18–25	26–30	31–35	Total
Sample size	563	342	346	1,251

Legend:
- Go alone
- Go with friends
- Go with family members

Source: ULI/Lachman Associates Survey, January 2013.
Note: Totals may not add up to 100 percent because of rounding.

FIGURE 7: Preferred Way to Shop for Own Clothes

Sample size: 1,251.

Source: ULI/Lachman Associates Survey, January 2013.
Definitions:
1. Macy's, Dillard's, Sears, JCPenney, Kohl's, etc.
2. Saks Fifth Avenue, Nordstrom, etc.
3. Walmart, Target, Kmart, Shopko, Meijer, etc.
4. Marshalls, T.J. Maxx, Ross Dress for Less, etc.

We asked how and where respondents prefer to shop for their own clothes. As figure 7 shows, 20 percent order clothing items online (22 percent of men versus 17 percent of women). Just 16 percent of men and 9 percent of women do online research before going to bricks-and-mortar stores that offer the clothing they want. One-fifth of respondents go directly to favorite branded stores; 19 percent go to a department store; 12 percent patronize a discount department store; and 10 percent visit an off-price store (e.g., Marshalls, T.J. Maxx, or Ross Dress for Less) for apparel purchases. In addition, 19 percent often patronize resale and consignment shops, and another 48 percent do so occasionally.

"I can't decide. I'm having a brand identity crisis."

Gen Y is brand conscious—not because they consider specific brands prestigious, but because they value consistent quality. This takes them to favorite branded stores and also explains online purchasing patterns; they use sites like J. Crew to lead them to "sanctioned" new products. Gen-Yers are suspicious about unknown brands and are unlikely to experiment without being able to touch and examine new products.

Grocery Shopping

Gen Y shops frequently for groceries. Although only 6 percent make a daily grocery purchase, 25 percent buy food more than twice a week and another 40 percent purchase groceries at least weekly. We first asked where respondents typically shop for nonperishable groceries (e.g., cereal, canned goods, paper products, pet food). Each person could mention up to three shopping venues, though more than 40 percent specified just one type of store. The results:

Walmart, Target, Kmart, Meijer, or other discount department store with a food section	63%
Supermarket	56%
Warehouse club (e.g., Costco, Sam's Club, BJ's)	23%
Discount supermarket (e.g., Aldi, Food 4 Less, Food Maxx)	20%
Small neighborhood grocery or food store	17%
Drugstore	5%
Online	1%

Clearly, Gen Y is cost-conscious: look at the heavy patronage of discount department stores, warehouse clubs, and discount supermarkets, all of which compete with traditional supermarkets. (There is a reason for the financial difficulties of SuperValu and A&P.) Two-thirds of suburban respondents cite traditional supermarkets, but they are the exceptional Gen-Yers.

Drugstores, which are popular among Gen Y, were included among the response options because they are expanding their nonperishable grocery sections and, in urban locations, are adding refrigerated and prepared foods. Only 5 percent of respondents included drugstores in their top three venues—but that proportion represents about 4 million Gen-Y grocery shoppers.

Online food shopping has not caught on yet, even for staple items. In Manhattan, Fresh Direct trucks deliver groceries constantly, but the buyer profile may be older than Gen Y. Young urbanites do not eat at home often enough to bother stocking groceries; take-out may suffice on the rare occasions when they are home for dinner. In all geographies, take-out is widely used. Casual suburban restaurants like Chili's, Macaroni Grill, and Ruby Tuesday often have designated parking spaces for customers picking up food to go, and supermarkets are liberally expanding their prepared-food and take-out sections.

Gen Y's purchasing profile for fresh groceries (fruits, vegetables, meats, dairy) is different from how they buy staples. Again, respondents could choose up to three venues, though only one-quarter did so; 30 percent mentioned two shopping sources; and the rest cited only one. The results for fresh grocery purchases are as follows:

Supermarket	61%
Walmart, Target, Kmart, Meijer, or other discount department store with a food section	49%
Specialty grocer (e.g., Whole Foods, Trader Joe's, natural food store, butcher)	18%
Small neighborhood grocery/food store	17%
Warehouse club	16%
Green grocer/farmers market	16%

For fresh items, supermarkets still outrank the discount department stores, where selections have only recently broadened. Meat, fish, and produce sections are being added to or enlarged in more of the smaller-format Walmarts and Targets. Supercenters that combine a full-size grocery with a discount department store are rising in popularity. Traditional supermarkets are especially popular for fresh foods in the East (76 percent) and in small towns and rural areas. Warehouse clubs are a competitive presence for fresh items as well as staples. They are mentioned by 29 percent of Gen-Yers in the West (Costco's home), but only by 20 to 21 percent in the other three regions. They are more popular in outlying suburbs (34 percent mention them) and least common in small towns (17 percent) and rural areas (18 percent), where distance may be a factor.

Online Shopping

Gen Y takes shopping seriously and spends a lot of online time researching, fantasizing, considering flash-sale promotions, checking out what celebrities are wearing and then imagining how they would look in similar outfits, using pinterest.com to share items with family members, and keeping up with food and fashion blogs. In fact, when asked how many hours they spend on line *per day* checking out retail-oriented sites, the response is:

	Total sample	Men	Women
Less than 1 hour	55%	52%	58%
1–2 hours	28%	28%	29%
2–3 hours	11%	12%	9%
>3 hours	6%	8%	4%

Again, this is *daily* computer time; 45 percent of respondents spend at least an hour each day on retail-oriented sites. Among those spending over two hours, men are more obsessed than women. Within Gen Y, male fashion has assumed a new prominence, and the overall survey results reinforce that trend.

Blessedly for mall owners, most Gen-Yers still prefer to buy in stores. As shown in figure 8, they may do product research and price comparisons online, but actual purchasing generally occurs in stores.

For cosmetics and personal-care products, 77 percent shop in stores. The proportion is 73 percent for shoes—though an additional 10 percent do research in stores and then buy online. For electronics, 38 percent purchase online, but, of those, one-quarter go to stores first to "showroom" the items and then buy online. Among those who acquire sporting goods—and 35 percent of respondents do not—45 percent buy online, often after examining the products in stores. As shown, Gen-Yers are savvy, careful shoppers; a great deal of research occurs online before store visits and vice versa.

"Gotta run, Sid! The cashmere everybody's been talking about is now twenty percent off!"

Use of mobile devices to compare prices while shopping in a store is becoming increasingly common. (For years, we read about this happening in tech-obsessed Japan and South Korea, but not in the United States.) Among Gen-Yers, 9 percent always do this type of price check and 18 percent often do so. Another 34 percent sometimes use their phones for competitive price verification. Once more, downtowners are the early adopters: 42 percent always or often use their cellphones to check prices. Our data mesh with those from an online consumer survey conducted by Harris Interactive Service Bureau for CouponCabin.com last September, which found that 43 percent of smartphone and tablet owners had engaged in "showrooming." Among the items showroomed,

FIGURE 8: **Preferred Way to Buy Selected Items**

	Electronics[1]	Shoes	Sports equipment/ accessories[2]	Cosmetics/ personal care items
Do my research and shopping only in stores	11%	48%	34%	57%
Do research online, but buy in a store	50%	25%	21%	20%
Do my research in stores, but then buy online	11%	10%	13%	8%
Buy online, without visiting a store	27%	17%	32%	15%

Sample size: 1,251.

Source: ULI/Lachman Associates Survey, January 2013.
Note: Totals may not add up to 100 percent because of rounding.
1. Computers, tablets, cellphones, TV/audio equipment, etc.
2. 35 percent of respondents do not buy these items; percentages are for those who do.

"50 percent of respondents said home electronics, while 44 percent said tech devices; . . . 40 percent said . . . entertainment items; 31 percent said . . . clothing; 29 percent said . . . shoes; and 24 percent said they showroomed computers."[8]

We asked how store pricing compares with online pricing for the same item. Here is Gen Y's assessment:

Store prices are always lower	6%
Store prices can be lower, but only if there's a sale or you have a coupon[9]	12%
It's a mixed bag: you won't know until you do research	54%
Online shopping can cost less, but only if free shipping is provided	20%
Online shopping always costs less	7%

Again, these are cost-conscious young people who know they have to evaluate pricing, whether online or in stores. And they do.

Gen-Y men are as active online shoppers as women, but their interests differ. Men are more likely to buy electronic and computer equipment, sporting goods, and liquor online; women predominate in purchases of children's items, housewares, cosmetics, books, gifts, and clothing. Tellingly, only 9 percent of both men and women purchased no goods whatsoever online in the six months before our survey. Among respondents in their early 30s (the older and wealthier Gen-Y contingent), the proportion making no online acquisitions is only 6 percent.

Not many respondents order food online for quick consumption, either from home or the office. We expected more use of mobile phones for lunch and dinner orders; but 68 percent of Gen-Yers say they rarely or never do this.

As online purchasing grows steadily, retailers struggle to find workable combinations of online and in-store sales and distribution:

- Some chain retailers, including department stores, encourage customers to pick up and/or return online orders at physical stores (to attract additional sales and reduce mailing costs).

- Purely online firms are opening showrooms so customers can see and feel their goods.

- Walmart is moving onto Amazon's turf as an online aggregator and distributor.

- Stores incorporate computer kiosks so shoppers can directly order out-of-stock sizes or colors (or items not carried in the stores at all) and have the goods sent to their homes. (Some Gen-Yers reject this process, saying they either buy the item at hand or they move on.)

- The issue of compensation for shipping costs (and returns) is unresolved.

- Many employers are not allowing workers to receive personal deliveries, which poses a problem for recipients if there is not a secure way to get deliveries at home.

- Payment of state sales tax for online transactions will become universal—but it is taking years and has given online retailers an advantage over physical stores.

To date, the big winners in this confused situation are Federal Express, the United Parcel Service, and the U.S. Postal Service, as well as warehouse owners and logistics/fulfillment firms. For industrial real estate owners and developers, the future is rosy. As national retailers adopt dual in-store/online sales strategies, they need two different types of warehouses. To stock their stores, they use traditional cross-docked facilities: trucks bring individual goods to one side of a regional warehouse; the shipment is broken up within the facility for delivery to specific stores; and trucks containing a mix of products drive off from the other side of the warehouse, heading for one or more stores. This is the usual logistics model for national retailers, with variation only in each chain's number and location of regional warehouses. The focus is generally on one-day driving times for final store deliveries.

Online fulfillment, however, requires different logistics: a highly automated pick-and-pack facility that sends out "onesies" and "twosies"—a pair of boots, one book, a cellphone, three bras, one dress shirt. Promised delivery times are shortening—to 24 hours or even same-day fulfillment. So far, this expensive approach is not adequately covered by delivery charges to purchasers. Warehouse owners are winning, as are online shoppers; but retailers are probably losing money in their attempts to accommodate patrons with just-in-time delivery.

FIGURE 9: Gen Y's Online/Wireless Shopping Habits

	Men	Women
Weekly online purchases[1]		
Under $50	45%	56%
$50–$99	15%	10%
$100–$299	15%	4%
Over $300	5%	3%
Rarely purchase items online	21%	26%
Do you use Facebook or Twitter to receive notices of upcoming sales, specials, or discounts?		
Yes	44%	54%
No	56%	46%
Do you have coupons or other special promotions sent to your cellphone?		
Yes	30%	38%
No	70%	62%
Have you ever bought items at an online flash sale?[2]		
Yes	41%	38%
No	59%	62%
Do you shop on eBay?		
Yes, occasionally	47%	43%
Yes, often	18%	12%
No	35%	44%
How did you shop for holiday gifts in 2012?		
Mainly online	29%	27%
Mainly in stores	36%	42%
A balance of both	35%	32%
Sample size	*617*	*634*

Source: ULI/Lachman Associates Survey, January 2013.
Note: Totals may not add up to 100 percent because of rounding.
1. Not including grocery items.
2. A special purchase or discount available for only a very limited time.

As reflected in figure 9, half of Gen-Yers spend less than $50 a week online. If the people who say they rarely buy online are eliminated, the proportion of actual online buyers spending under $50 per week rises to two-thirds. On the other hand, 13 percent of the serious shoppers—10 million Gen-Yers—spend $100 to $300 a week online, and another 5 percent say they buy more than $300 in nongrocery items per week. Those are meaningful acquisitions, and men constitute more of the serious spenders.

Women have the edge in using social networking to learn about online discounts or specials, but men pay attention to flash sales and are more inclined to shop on eBay.

Dining and Entertainment

Like all Americans, Gen-Yers eat out frequently, especially for lunch and dinner. As figure 10 shows, 38 percent of the sample reports having at least one dinner a week in a restaurant and 36 percent eat lunch out with the same frequency. For men, the proportions are considerably higher: 45 percent and 44 percent, respectively. Although only 22 percent of the sample eat breakfast out one or more times a week, that still adds up to a minimum of 17.6 million morning meals eaten away from home by members of Generation Y.

Having dinner out is very popular: 80 percent go out for an evening meal multiple times a month. Only one-fifth say they rarely or never eat dinner out. Over half of Gen-Yers living downtown enjoy restaurant dinners at least once a week, whereas only a quarter of rural dwellers do the same. Availability of more and varied dining choices undoubtedly accounts for the greater restaurant patronage among downtowners. Our focus group—downtowners all—felt that eating out could be less expensive than buying groceries to eat in because food can spoil when plans change.

Even though being served costs more, this generation likes it. Because dining out is one of Gen-Yers' primary social activities, table service is preferred.

Hispanics eat out most frequently, with 52 percent saying they dine out with their spouse/partner and/or friends at least once a week (as compared with 46 percent for the survey as a whole). Hispanics' propensity to go out for weekend brunch is especially notable. Brunch is also more popular in the South, where 20 percent go weekly, and among downtown residents, with one-third saying they go for brunch each weekend.

Four of ten survey respondents prefer to patronize independent neighborhood restaurants when they go out for dinner, and another 41 percent choose a chain restaurant, be it with or without table service. However, 12 percent prefer "hot" new places, moving on constantly to the latest trendy spot.[10] (Downtowners skew this figure, because 21 percent of them favor new places. Also, Hispanics lean toward hot restaurants.)

Nearly half of the survey respondents say they frequently combine a shopping trip with a meal out, and another 47 percent sometimes do so. Only 6 percent say they never eat out as part of a shopping trip. Again, this reinforces the view that Gen Y considers the shopping experience to be entertaining, fun, and sharable.

Generation Y:
SHOPPING AND ENTERTAINMENT
IN THE DIGITAL AGE

FIGURE 10: Dining Out

	GENDER			RACE/ ETHNICITY	
	Men	Women	Total	Hispanic	Black
How often do you eat out for . . . ?					
Breakfast					
At least once a week	28%	15%	22%	31%	34%
A few times a month	18%	15%	16%	20%	18%
Rarely or never	54%	70%	62%	50%	48%
Lunch					
At least once a week	44%	28%	36%	45%	43%
A few times a month	32%	38%	35%	32%	32%
Rarely or never	25%	34%	29%	23%	25%
Dinner					
At least once a week	45%	31%	38%	47%	39%
A few times a month	35%	48%	42%	36%	40%
Rarely or never	20%	20%	20%	16%	20%
Weekend brunch					
At least once a week	22%	11%	16%	25%	24%
A few times a month	19%	15%	17%	20%	19%
Rarely or never	59%	74%	67%	54%	57%
How often do you eat out with your spouse/partner and/or friends?					
Daily	11%	5%	8%	11%	9%
Several times a week	23%	13%	18%	22%	18%
Once a week	20%	20%	20%	19%	20%
A couple of times a month	28%	34%	31%	28%	26%
Just a few times a year	19%	27%	23%	19%	27%
Preferred place to go out for dinner					
Hot new restaurant	13%	10%	12%	17%	14%
Favorite local or neighborhood place	44%	37%	40%	40%	28%
Casual chain restaurant with table service	27%	35%	31%	27%	38%
Quick/casual place[1]	8%	12%	10%	9%	11%
Fast-food place[2]	8%	7%	7%	6%	10%
Sample size	*617*	*634*	*1,251*	*255*	*198*

Source: ULI/Lachman Associates Survey, January 2013.
Note: Totals may not add up to 100 percent because of rounding.
Definitions:
1. Panera, Cosi, Chipotle, Fazoli, Qdoba, Five Guys, or similar.
2. Wendy's, McDonald's, Burger King, Taco Bell, Carl's Jr., Sonic, or similar.

Free-Time Activities

Gen-Yers' favorite ways of using free time are shown in figure 11. For men, watching TV ranks first, followed by listening to/playing music and playing computer games. Spending time with friends is a close fourth. Most popular for women is spending time with family, followed by watching television and reading. Again, spending time with friends ranks fourth.

FIGURE 11: Most Frequent Uses of Free Time

	Men	Women
Watch TV	58%	54%
Spend time with family	38%	57%
Read	29%	47%
Listen to/play music	43%	39%
Spend time with friends	41%	43%
Play computer games	42%	21%
Online social networking	28%	33%
Cooking	16%	29%
Go to the gym, exercise, indoor sports	25%	17%
Shop in stores	11%	24%
Shop online	16%	21%
Sample size	617	634

Source: ULI/Lachman Associates Survey, January 2013.
Note: Activities listed were cited by at least 20 percent of the total sample. Respondents could check up to five activities.

The draw of friends and family for Gen Y cannot be overstated: most had happy childhoods and remain closely tied to their families and their friends' families. As one pundit says, "It's not about keeping up with the Joneses; it's about hanging with the Jones family." In figure 11, "online social networking" could well be added to the time spent with relatives and peers. (Recall that 37 percent of survey respondents prefer to shop for clothes with family members, and another 28 percent do so with friends.)

One-quarter of men and 17 percent of women go to gyms and/or exercise classes and/or participate in indoor sports. In our focus group at Columbia Business School, participants thought that gyms, with their juice bars, could become Starbucks-like gathering places. The graduate students coordinate yoga classes and gym visits with friends, sometimes followed by group appointments at Dry Bar to fix their hair and prepare for an evening out.

The roles played by restaurants, bars, shopping centers, and coffee shops in Gen-Y gatherings with friends are highlighted in figure 12. When asked where they prefer to get together with friends, a private home ranks first for everyone except downtown residents, for whom restaurants are cited first. Six of ten Gen-Yers love to gather at restaurants. More men than women favor bars, but the reverse is true for shopping centers. Also, 24 percent of men cite "sports events" as favorite places to congregate with friends.

Movie-going is a popular social activity for three-fourths of survey respondents. Of those, seven of ten men and more than half of the women see at least 12 movies in a theater per year. Not surprisingly, younger Gen-Yers go to movies more often than those in their 30s. A concern mentioned by some respondents was the cost of going to the movies, particularly if it required hiring a baby-sitter.

Almost two-thirds of respondents—69 percent of men and 57 percent of women—patronize music, dance, and comedy clubs. However, as shown in figure 12, most go infrequently.

FIGURE 12: Gen Y's Social Activities

Favorite places to get together with friends

	Percentage
At home—my place or theirs	66%
At a restaurant	59%
At a bar	30%
At a shopping center	28%
At a coffee shop	22%
At a park/the beach	20%

Sample size: 1,251.

Note: Places listed were cited by at least 20 percent of the total sample. Each respondent could select up to three places.

Movie-going

75% go out to the movies

	MOVIE-GOERS	
	Men	Women
Attendance frequency		
At least once a week	12%	5%
Couple of times a month	32%	22%
Once a month	26%	26%
Less than once a month	30%	47%
Sample size	*452*	*471*

Clubbing

63% go out to clubs—but not often. Of those who do:

Attendance frequency	
At least once a week	9%
Couple of times a month	16%
Once a month	19%
Less than once a month	55%

Sample size: 786.

Source: ULI/Lachman Associates Survey, January 2013.
Note: Totals may not add up to 100 percent because of rounding.

Rent versus Buy

Much has been written about Gen Y's "sharing economy," emphasizing their focus on instant gratification and therefore an inclination to rent rather than own everything from cars to wedding dresses. As with many assertions, there is some evidence but not universal concurrence on this subject. Our survey points to fewer rentals of goods than expected, though men are somewhat more inclined than women to try renting.

Among the choices listed in the survey, the strongest response was for rental of fancy clothes for parties or weddings; but three-fourths of Gen-Yers (and 88 percent of women) have never done this. For men, a traditional rental is a tuxedo for a formal event; for women, renting a party dress is a newer phenomenon. Nonetheless, extrapolating from our sample, more than 18 million people between 18 and 35 have rented such clothes, and half of them would do so again. Somewhat surprisingly, one-fifth of Gen-Y males have rented business clothes for interviews or special meetings/presentations. They might not have contracted for complete outfits, as one can simply rent a luxurious silk tie to create a sophisticated impression for a week or so.

"How can we know who we are when the best marketing consultants of our time don't know."

Only 24 percent of males and 13 percent of females have rented tools—but keep in mind that one-fourth of Gen-Yers live at home or school; 37 percent rent their dwellings; and among the 32 percent who own their residences, many have condominium units without yards. Even so, the thesis in Gen-Y literature is that, unlike Baby Boomers, Millennials do not want to acquire tools for occasional use and will rent instead. Home Depot is said to be expanding its tool rental program, and that seems sensible—though our data do not provide resounding support. Demand may rise as Gen Y matures, however.

Car sharing is different. Zipcar and similar programs are gradually expanding to more locations, primarily in central cities, and use is accelerating. Pilot sharing programs are popping up in suburban neighborhoods as well. Not quite one-third of respondents are aware of car sharing systems in their communities and, among those, one-quarter avail themselves of the programs. Not surprisingly, patronage is heaviest among downtowners, followed by residents of newer suburbs. The former makes perfect sense because car sharing began in central cities and fewer downtown denizens own automobiles. Use by suburbanites may actually be a stronger indication of this generation's values.

Gen Y's view of automobiles is utilitarian: compared with prior generations, they acquire driver's licenses later and they drive far fewer miles per year. Three-fourths of respondents have cars; however, an RCLCO survey conducted last fall in America's 20 largest metropolitan areas revealed that almost one-fifth of Gen-Yers "would consider giving up the cars they own, because the cost of ownership is not justified by the amount they use it."[11] Many Gen-Yers like to walk, ride bikes, take public transit, drive hybrids, and share cars—not particularly good news for the auto industry, but a vote in favor of densification.

In *Time* last September, Roya Wolverson observed that the Facebook age is "one that prioritizes impermanence and immediacy, which also breeds a renter mentality."[12] If you are into the continuously fresh, rental is the answer: you wear the dress, drive the car, hang the modern art, give your child a toy, and then return everything when the lease is up. Next time will be a new adventure. The perfect metaphor is the online company called Mine for Nine: maternity rentals.

Notes

1. Our survey was administered by Harris Interactive Service Bureau; the methodology is described in the Appendix.

2. M. Leanne Lachman and Deborah L. Brett, *Generation Y: America's New Housing Wave*, Urban Land Institute, 2011, p. 15.

3. Annie Lowrey, "When Problems Start Getting Real . . ." *New York Times Magazine*, March 31, 2013, p. 13 (posted online, March 26, 2013, under title "Do Millennials Stand a Chance in the Real World?").

4. Larissa Faw, "Meet the Millennial 1 Percent: Young, Rich, and Redefining Luxury," *ForbesWoman*, October 2, 2012.

5. Many respondents are still in school and therefore may incur new or additional indebtedness before completing their educations.

6. *Young Adults After the Recession: Fewer Homes, Fewer Cars, Less Debt*, Pew Research Center, Washington, D.C., February 21, 2013.

7. Neil Shah, "Young Adults Retreat from Piling Up Debt," *Wall Street Journal*, March 4, 2013.

8. "Study: More than 40 Percent of Smartphone and Tablet Owners 'Showroom,' " *Chain Store Age*, October 20, 2012.

9. Half of all respondents purchase discount coupons from Groupon, Living Social, etc. Many are for restaurants and services, but some are for stores. Among purchasers, the vast majority say the discounts encourage patronage of facilities that are new to them.

10. A "hot" restaurant can be especially appealing when it does not take reservations or has a complicated advanced-booking system. Some Gen-Yers say it's fun to wait up to two hours at a nearby bar with a crowd of friends before getting into a coveted dining spot.

11. RCLCO, *The Advisory*, December 3, 2012, p. 2.

12. Roya Wolverson, "Rental Nation," *Time*, September 24, 2012, p. 52.

Appendix: Survey Methodology

To understand Gen Y's shopping habits and dining/entertainment preferences, Lachman Associates LLC designed an online survey administered by Harris Interactive Service Bureau to a nationally representative panel of Americans ages 18 to 35. The panel was selected to reflect Gen Y's age distribution (18–25, 26–30, and 31–35 in 2013), gender, race, Hispanic ethnicity, and geographic distribution among the country's four regions as defined by the U.S. Census Bureau. The targets for panel selection were based on the demographic characteristics of Gen-Yers as shown in July 1, 2011, U.S. Census Bureau estimates.[1] The figure below shows how the final sample (1,251 respondents) compared with the census targets. As indicated, the sample closely reflects Gen Y's composition. Statistical analyses found that, in every case, the observed difference in percentages fell well within the 90 percent confidence interval.

Sample Design Parameters and Actual Respondent Demographics

	Completed survey respondents	2011 U.S. Census Bureau estimates	Difference	Confidence intervals (90%, two-tailed)
Gender				
Male	49.3%	50.7%	-1.4%	+/-2.3%
Female	50.7%	49.3%	+1.4%	+/-2.3%
Age				
18–25	45.0%	45.9%	-0.9%	+/-2.3%
26–30	27.3%	27.6%	-0.2%	+/-2.1%
31–35	27.7%	26.6%	+1.1%	+/-2.1%
Race				
White alone	74.3%	75.3%	-1.0%	+/-2.0%
Black alone	15.8%	14.7%	+1.1%	+/-1.7%
All other	9.9%	10.0%	-0.1%	+/-1.4%
Hispanic origin				
Hispanic	20.4%	20.5%	-0.2%	+/-1.9%
Not Hispanic	79.6%	79.5%	0.2%	+/-1.9%
Region				
Northeast	17.3%	17.4%	-0.1%	+/-1.8%
Midwest	20.7%	21.0%	-0.3%	+/-1.9%
South	37.7%	37.2%	+0.5%	+/-2.3%
West	24.3%	24.4%	-0.1%	+/-2.0%

Sources: Lachman Associates LLC; Harris Interactive Service Bureau.
Note: Totals may not add up to 100 percent because of rounding.

Prior to designing the survey, the authors conducted a focus group with students at Columbia University's Graduate School of Business to provide insights into how Gen-Yers shop, what their free-time activities are, how they patronize restaurants and movie theaters, and—most important—how they use digital media to stay abreast of the latest fashion trends, do research before visiting stores or making online purchases, compare prices, and share their plans with friends.

The online survey was conducted between January 22 and February 1, 2013. Respondents were required to answer all questions, with the exception of those pertaining to household income and anticipated earnings in 2013 for those employed full time.[2] Harris Interactive Service Bureau tabulated the results.

Because the sample represents Gen Y as a whole, the youngest participants include men and women who never completed high school, are recent high school graduates, or are still finishing their undergraduate educations. At the older end, it includes Gen-Yers who have been in the workforce for ten to 15 years or more. It includes single people who live alone or with roommates or who still reside with their parents, as well as families with children. As befits an 18-year generation of Americans, this is a diverse group with wide-ranging opinions about everything—and they are eager to share their views.

Notes

1. http://www.census.gov/popest/data/state/asrh/2011/index.html.
2. Only 7 percent of respondents declined to provide household income data; 3 percent declined to provide anticipated 2013 earnings.